G U I D E S

HTML5 TO THE POINT

Quick solutions to all of your HTML5 questions — comprehensive and to the point!

by **Scott DeLoach**

HTML 5 *to the point*
Scott DeLoach

www.clickstart.net

Design: Patrick Hofmann
Cover: Laura Suarez
Copy Edit: Phil Duris

ISBN: 978-0-578-06654-7

9 8 7 6 5 4 3 2 1

Printed and bound in the United States of America

Dedication

This book is dedicated to my friends. Thanks for making life fun.

May misfortune follow you the rest of your life, and never catch up.

Contents

Structure 41

Format   51

Forms   59

Images, Videos, and Sounds   71

Introduction

This book was designed to help you find quick solutions to common HTML5 questions. The sections use a question-answer format, with a short description of the question, a visual example, and the HTML5 solution.

Icons used in this book

The following icons are used throughout this book to help you find important and time-saving information.

Icon	Meaning	Description
⚠	Caution	Information about feature that may be removed from HTML5.
◇	Note	Additional information about a topic.
TIP▶	Tip	A recommended best practice, shortcut, or workaround.

Updates

For the most up-to-date information about this book, see www.clickstart.net or www.html5tothepoint.com.

Overview

This section provides a focused, "to the point" overview of HTML5.

What is HTML5?

HTML5 is a new version of HTML4 and XHTML1 that also adds new APIs for Web applications. Other specifications, such as SVG, Geolocation, and WAI-ARIA, are often grouped with HTML5 even though they are not part of HTML5. This book also covers SVG, Geolocation, and WAI-ARIA so you can use them in your HTML5 documents.

The W3C started developing HTML5 in 2004. It is being developed as a joint effort between the W3C HTML Working Group and the Web Hypertext Application Technology Working Group (WHATWG).

Why did the W3C create HTML5?

According to the W3C, HTML5 "reflects an effort, started in 2004, to study contemporary HTML implementations and deployed content. The HTML5 draft:

- Defines a single language called HTML5 which can be written in HTML or XHTML syntax (or 'serialization').

- Defines detailed processing models to foster interoperable implementations.

- Improves markup for documents.

- Introduces markup and APIs for emerging idioms, such as Web applications."

How did they select the new elements for HTML5?

Ian Hickson, the editor of the HTML 5 recommendation for WHATWG, analyzed over a **billion** web pages to determine the most commonly-used class names. Authors often use classes to tag blocks of content, such as headers, that have a specific purpose and/or require unique formatting. The top twenty class names were:

❑ footer	❑ main
❑ menu	❑ search
❑ title	❑ msonormal
❑ small	❑ date
❑ text	❑ smalltext
❑ content	❑ body
❑ header	❑ style1
❑ nav	❑ top
❑ copyright	❑ white
❑ button	❑ link

Some of these classes, such as "msonormal" (often created by Microsoft Office when you save an Office document as html), "smalltext," "style1," and "white," are format-specific or meaningless. The other classes match the new HTML5 elements as follows:

Class	HTML5 Element
footer	footer
menu	menu
title header top	header
small smalltext	small
text content main body	article
nav	nav

Class	HTML5 Element
copyright	none
search	none
date	date

Who is the editor of the HTML5 recommendation?

Ian Hickson (@hixie) is the editor of the HTML5 recommendation for the W3C. Dave Hyatt, the co-creator of Firefox, helped Ian Hickson develop the HTML5 recommendation.

Does HTML5 replace HTML4?

Yes.

HTML4 is very forgiving, but the code is often unorganized. HTML5 adds new structure elements such as section, article, and nav to help organize content.

Does HTML5 replace XHTML?

Yes. The W3C has stated that they are no longer developing XHTML 2. As Tim Berners Lee announced in 2006, "The attempt to get the world to switch to XML, including quotes around attribute values and slashes in empty tags and namespaces all at once didn't work."

Which browsers support HTML5?

Currently, no browser provides complete support for HTML5.

For an up-to-date summary of browser support for HTML5's new elements, attributes, APIs, and other features, see any of the following sites:

- en.wikipedia.org/wiki/Comparison_of_layout_engines_(HTML_5)

- www.caniuse.com

- www.quirksmode.org/dom/html5.html

To test your browser's support for HTML5, see www.html5test.com.

Do mobile devices support HTML5?

Yes. iPhone/iPad, Android, and Palm Pre devices all support browsers that are based on the Webkit rendering engine, which supports HTML5.

For more information about using HTML5 on mobile devices or developing HTML5 applications for mobile applications, see Ian Sefferman's website www.mobilehtml5.com.

How can I emulate mobile devices for testing?

You can use Safari to see how your page will appear in mobile devices or other browsers.

1. Open Safari.

2. Select **Edit** > **Preferences** > **Advanced**.

3. Select the **Show Develop menu in toolbar** checkbox.

4. Select **Develop** > **User Agent**.

TIP *To mimic the iPhone, set the maximum width of your document to 480px and use the Helvetica font.*

Can I make HTML5 work in older browsers?

Older browsers may not support XHTML, so you should use the HTML syntax. You will also need to provide style definitions for the new elements in HTML5.

Example

article,aside,canvas,details,figcaption,figure,footer,header,hgroup,menu,nav,section, summary { display: block; }

Can I make HTML5 work with Internet Explorer?

Yes!

Remy Sharp has written a JavaScript that you can use to make HTML5 elements work in Internet Explorer 8 and below. See www.remysharp.com/2009/01/07/html5-enabling-script.

What does HTML5's syntax look like?

There are two syntaxes that can be used to for HTML5 documents: HTML-based syntax and XHTML-based syntax.

To use HTML syntax, you should include the DOCTYPE declaration (case insensitive).

Example HTML Syntax

```
<!DOCTYPE html>
<html>
 <head>...</head>
 <body>... </body>
</html>
```

To use XHTML syntax, you must specify the XML namespace for the html element. The DOCTYPE declaration is optional. If you include it, "DOCTYPE" must be uppercase. "html" is case insensitive.

Example XHTML Syntax

```
<html xmlns="http://www.w3.org/1999/xhtml>
 <head>...</head>
 <body>... </body>
</html>
```

What are the advantages of using HTML syntax?

The HTML syntax has the following advantages:

- It's backward compatible with existing browsers

- More authors are familiar with HTML than XHTML syntax

- You can omit some tags and attribute values

Since the HTML-based syntax is more forgiving and better supported by browsers, it's a safe choice until support for HTML5 is more widespread.

What are the advantages of using XHTML syntax?

The XHTML syntax has the following advantages:

- It requires well-formed markup, which is easier to maintain

- It integrates directly with SVG and MathML

The downside of using the XHTML syntax is that all of your code has to be written correctly. If you make one mistake in a XHTML-based document, it will not display.

What is the HTML5 DOCTYPE declaration?

HTML5's DOCTYPE declaration is:

```
<!DOCTYPE html>
```

For HTML5 using HTML syntax, the DOCTYPE is not case sensitive, but it is usually written as capitalized above. If a browser or web server requires a DOCTYPE, you can use:

```
<!DOCTYPE html SYSTEM "about:legacy-compat">
```

The capitalization must match the example, and you must use double quotes.

For HTML5 using XHTML syntax, the DOCTYPE is optional and case sensitive. If you include it, it triggers "no-quirks" mode.

If a browser or webserver requires a DOCTYPE, you can use:

```
<!DOCTYPE html SYSTEM 'about:legacy-compat'>
```

The capitalization must match the example, and you must use single quotes. The quotes are used to distinguish between HTML and XHTML syntax.

What is quirks mode?

There are three rendering modes in HTML5: the default no quirks mode (aka "standards" or "strict" mode), limited quirks mode (aka "almost standards" mode), and quirks mode. Quirks mode is used to provide backwards compatibility with older browsers. Since browsers provide widely varying support for standards, quirks mode produces different results in each browser. The browsers even use different names for the modes!

If you use the <!DOCTYPE html> declaration, the browser will use "no quirks" mode. If you do not use a DOCTYPE declaration, older browsers will use quirks mode.

For a detailed discussion of rendering modes and their differences, see Henri Sivonen's website at hsivonen.iki.fi/doctype.

Should I close empty elements?

HTML5's HTML-based syntax does not require you to close empty or 'void' elements such as input, br, and img. So, <br> and <br /> are both valid. If you are using the XHTML-based syntax, you should to close empty elements because it is required in XHTML.

Does WordPress support HTML5?

Yes.

There are many HTML5 WordPress themes available at www.socialblogr.com/2010/03/8-free-html5-wordpress-themes.html and digwp.com/2009/07/free-html-5-wordpress-theme.

Can I use MathML with HTML5?

Yes, but browsers currently provide very limited support for MathML.

A good test of MathML support in your browser can be found at eyeasme.com/Joe/MathML/HTML5_MathML_browser_test.html

Moving to HTML5

How do I convert to HTML5?

Converting to HTML5 is more complex than selecting "Save as HTML5" in an application. To convert to HTML5, you will need to:

Task	See Page
Change your DOCTYPE	14
Replace any unsupported elements	27
Add the new structure elements	41

If you are not ready to convert, you can prepare for the conversion by using HTML5's elements as class names. This approach will make converting much easier, and it will help you get used to the new structure elements. For an example of using HTML5 elements as class names, see Jon Tan's post at www.jontangerine.com/log/2008/03/ preparing-for-html5-with-semantic-class-names.

Which HTML4 elements are supported?

The following HTML4 elements are supported in HTML5:

Element	Short Description
a	Hyperlink
abbr	Abbreviation
address	Contact information
area	Image map region
b	Boldfaced text

Element	Short Description
base	Base URL for relative links in a page
bdo	Bi-directional text override
blockquote	Long quotation
body	Main content
br	Line break
button	Button
caption	Table caption
cite	Title of a work, such as a book or painting.
code	Code fragment
col	Table column
colgroup	Table column group
dd	Description of an item in a definition list (dl)
del	Deletion
dfn	Definition of a term
div	Generic division
dl	Definition list
dt	Definition term
em	Emphasis
fieldset	Form control
form	Form for user input
h1-h6	Heading level 1-6

Element	Short Description
head	Document head
hr	Horizontal rule (i.e., a line)
html	Document root
i	Italicized text
iframe	Inline frame
img	Image
input	Form control
ins	Inserted text
kbd	Text to be typed by the user ('keyboard')
label	Input element label
legend	Fieldset caption
li	List item
link	Link to a resource such as a stylesheet
map	Client-side image map
meta	Information about the document ('metadata')
noscript	Alternative content for no script support
object	Generic embedded resource
ol	Ordered list
optgroup	Option group in a select list
option	An option in a select list
p	Paragraph

Element	Short Description
param	Parameters for an object or applet
pre	Preformatted text
q	Inline quotation
samp	Sample code output
script	Linked or embedded script
select	Selection (i.e., drop-down) list
small	Small print
span	Generic inline container
strong	Strong importance
style	Embedded styles declaration block
sub	Subscript
sup	Superscript
table	Table
tbody	Table body
td	Table data cell
textarea	Multi-line text box
tfoot	Table footer
th	Table header cell
thead	Table head
title	Document title
tr	Table row

Element	Short Description
ul	Unordered (i.e., bulleted) list
var	Variable

What are the new elements?

The following elements are new in HTML5:

Element	Short Description	See Page
article	A block of content that might be syndicated.	42
aside	Content that is either related to the content surrounding it or the site as a whole.	46
audio	Inserts an audio file.	51
canvas	Creates an area for images and shapes.	73
command	Defines a command that can be reused as needed.	87
datagrid	Displays information as a tree, list, or table. ⚠️ *The datagrid element may be removed from HTML5.*	54
datalist	Adds autocomplete options for a textbox.	55
details	Shows and hides content.	85
dialog	Indicates a quoted conversation. ⚠️ *The dialog element may be removed from HTML5.*	56
embed	Inserts an application or interactive content.	84
eventsource	Specifies an external source for a script or a web-based application.	87
figcaption	A caption for a figure.	47
figure	Content that is referenced from the main content but could be moved to the side of the page.	47

Element	Short Description	See Page
footer	An author's name, links to related documents, or a copyright statement.	45
header	A document or section heading, a section's table of contents, a search form, or a logo.	41
hgroup	Groups a heading with subheadings, an alternative title, and/or a tagline.	44
keygen	Generates a public-private key pair.	69
mark	Emphasized content in a quote that was not emphasized by the original author, or emphasized content that is most likely relevant to the user.	53
menu	Creates a toolbar, context menu, or list of commands.	87
meter	Allows a user to select an amount within a set range.	89
nav	Indicates a document's primary navigation links.	47
optgroup	Groups items in a drop-down listbox.	65
output	Displays the results of a calculation.	89
progress	Indicates when an event will be completed.	89
ruby rt rp	Adds pronunciation guides to content.	95
section	A self-contained block of content.	41
source	An alternate audio or video file.	78
summary	The legend (i.e., title) of a details element.	86
time	Specifies a date and time.	55
video	Inserts a video file.	78
wbr	A line break "opportunity"	54

The input element's type attribute has the following new values:

Attribute	Use	Sample Appearance
color	Selecting a color.	
date	Selecting a date (year, month, day) without a time zone.	
datetime	Selecting the time, with the time zone offset from UTC.	

Attribute	Use	Sample Appearance
datetime-local	Selecting the local date and time (year, month, day, hour, minute, second, fraction of a second) without a time zone.	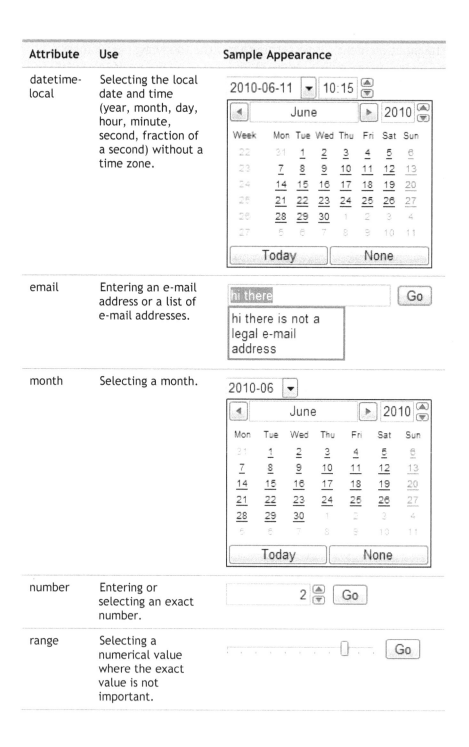
email	Entering an e-mail address or a list of e-mail addresses.	
month	Selecting a month.	
number	Entering or selecting an exact number.	
range	Selecting a numerical value where the exact value is not important.	

Attribute	Use	Sample Appearance
search	Entering text. The search type can have a unique design, or it can be identical to the text type.	
tel	Entering a phone number.	
time	Selecting a time (hour, minute, seconds, fractional seconds) without a time zone.	10:15 ⏶⏷ [Go]
url	Entering an absolute URL.	guten tag [Go] guten tag is not a valid Web address
week	Selecting a week-year number and a week number with no time zone.	2010-W28 ▾ ◄ July ► 2010 ⏶⏷ Week Mon Tue Wed Thu Fri Sat Sun 26 28 29 30 1 2 3 4 27 5 6 7 8 9 10 11 28 12 13 14 15 16 17 18 29 19 20 21 22 23 24 25 30 26 27 28 29 30 31 1 31 2 3 4 5 6 7 8 [Today] [None]

Which elements have changed from HTML4?

The following elements have been slightly modified to match how they are actually used and/or to make them more useful:

Element	What's Changed
a	An a element without an href attribute now represents a "placeholder link."
address	Redefined to be used only for contact information for an article, section, or entire document.
b	Text that should be "stylistically offset" but without any extra importance, such as keywords or product names. The b element does not mean something will necessarily appear as boldface.
cite	The title of a work. It should not be used for an author or individual's name.
hr	A paragraph-level thematic break.
i	Text in an alternate voice or mood, or otherwise "stylistically offset," such as a technical term, a phrase in another language, a ship name. The i element does not mean something will necessarily appear as italicized.
iframe	The new seamless attribute allows the inline frame to appear as part of the containing document without borders or scrollbars.
label	Focus should no longer move from the label to the form control unless such behavior is standard for the viewing device's user interface.
menu	Redefined to be used for toolbars and context menus.
small	Represents small print for side comments and legal text.
strong	Represents importance rather than strong emphasis or boldfacing.

Which elements are not supported?

The following elements have been removed in HTML5:

Element	HTML5 Alternative
acronym	Use the abbr element.
applet	Use the object element.
basefont	Use CSS (define the body element's style properties).
bgsound	Use the audio element.
big	Use CSS (font-size property).
center	Use CSS (text-align: center).
dir	Use ul.
font	Use CSS (font properties)
frame frameset noframes	Use an iframe or CSS (float properties).
listing	Use the pre element.
marquee	Use an animated image, a script, or the canvas element.
nobr	Use CSS (white-space: nowrap).
isindex	Use a form with a text input and submit button.
dir	Use the ul element.
noembed	The video element provides a simpler alternative.
noscript	Only conforms to HTML5's HTML syntax. It is not included in the XML syntax because it relies on an HTML parser.
plaintext	Use the pre element.
s strike	Use the del element or CSS (text-decoration: line-through).
spacer	Use CSS or possibly an empty div element.
tt	Use the code element or CSS (use a mono-space font).
u	Use CSS (text-decoration: underline).
xmp	Use the pre element.

What are the new attributes?

The following table summarizes the new attributes in HTML5:

Element	Attribute	Description
all	class	Specifies a style class (or a list of classes) that should be used to format the element.
	dir	Specifies the element's text direction: ltr (left-to-right) or rtl (right-to-left).
	id	A unique identifier for the element.
	lang	Specifies the element's language. For a list of valid values, see www.iana.org/assignments/language-subtag-registry.
	style	Specifies formatting to be applied to the element.
all (cont)	tabindex	Enables the element to receive focus and adds it to the tab list.
	title	Specifies tooltip text or titles or descriptions for links and images.
a	media	Added for consistency with the link element.
	ping	Specifies a space-separated list of URLs that will be 'pinged' when the hyperlink is followed. The ping attribute can allow users to know which URLs are going to be pinged so that they can turn it off.
	target	Deprecated in strict HTML4, but valid for use with iframes in HTML5.
area	media	Added for consistency with the link element.
	ping	Specifies a space-separated list of URLs that will be 'pinged' when the hyperlink is followed. The ping attribute can allow users to know which URLs are going to be pinged so that they can turn it off.
	target	Deprecated in strict HTML4, but valid for use with iframes in HTML5.
	hreflang	Added for consistency with the a and link elements.

Element	Attribute	Description
area (cont)	rel	Added for consistency with the a and link elements.
base	target	Added for consistency with the a element.
li	value	Deprecated in HTML4, but valid for use in numbered lists (ol element) in HTML5.
ol	start	Deprecated in HTML4, but valid in HTML5.
	reversed	Indicates that the list numbering should descend (i.e., 3, 2, 1).
meta	charset	Specifies the document's character encoding.
textarea	placeholder	Specifies temporary text that will disappear when the element receives focus.
textarea (cont)	autofocus	Gives the form element focus when the page loads.
	required	Indicates that the user has to provide a value to submit the form.
	form	Associates a form element with a form. Form elements can now be be placed anywhere on a page.
select	autofocus	Gives the form element focus when the page loads.
	form	Associates a form element with a form. Form elements can now be be placed anywhere on a page.
input	placeholder	Specifies temporary text that will appear in the element and disappear when it receives focus.
	autocomplete	Specifies that the value can be stored and auto-filled when the user returns to the page.
	autofocus	Gives the form element focus when the page loads.
	form	Associates a form element with a form. Form elements can now be be placed anywhere on a page.

Element	Attribute	Description
input (cont)	formaction formenctype formmethod formnovalidate formtarget	If present, these attributes override the action, enctype, method, novalidate, and target attributes.
	list	Specifies a datalist to be used for the available options.
	min max	Specify the minimum and maximum allowed values.
	multiple	Allows the user to select multiple values.
	pattern	Specifies a regular expression that will be used to check the element's value.
	required	Indicates that the user has to provide a value to submit the form.
	step	Limits the number of allowed values between the min and max. For example, a step of 2 with a min of 1 and a max of 5 would limit the values to 1, 3, and 5.
output	form	Associates a form element with a form. Form elements can now be be placed anywhere on a page.
button	formaction formenctype formmethod formnovalidate formtarget	If present, these attributes override the action, enctype, method, novalidate, and target attributes.
	form	Associates a form element with a form. Form elements can now be be placed anywhere on a page.
	autofocus	Gives the form element focus when the page loads.

Element	Attribute	Description
fieldset	disabled	Disables the elements inside the fieldset.
	form	Associates a form element with a form. Form elements can now be be placed anywhere on a page.
form	novalidate	Disables form validation submission (i.e., the form can always be submitted).
menu	type	Specifies that the element should appear as a menu or as a context menu if the contextmenu attribute is being used.
	label	Specifies a label for the menu.
style	scoped	Applies style definitions to an element rather than the entire document. The scoped attribute is required if the style element is used outside of the document's head.
script	async	Specifies whether a script will run:
	defer	▫ async – the script loads and run asynchronously as the page continues loading
		▫ defer – the script loads and runs after the page loads
html	manifest	Points to an application cache manifest used in conjunction with the API for offline Web applications.
link	sizes	Can be used with the rel attribute to indicate the size of the referenced icon. If specified, the icon typically appears on the document's tab in a browser.
iframe	sandbox	Can be used to make an iframe more secure.
	seamless	Allows the inline frame to appear as part of the containing document, without borders or scrollbars.
	srcdoc	Specifies code (including a link that can open a document) that will appear in the iframe.

What are the new global attributes?

The following global attributes are new in HTML5:

Name	Definition
contenteditable	Allows the user to edit an element (but not save it without addition scripting).
contextmenu	Creates a popup menu.
draggable	Allows an element to be moved.
hidden	Hides the element. Similar to using display: hidden, but the hidden attribute can be used by screen readers.
item	Adds the element as an item in a specified menu.
spellcheck	Spellchecks the element's text (very useful for editable elements).

Which attributes should not be used?

The following attributes are allowed in HTML5, but you should avoid using them:

Element	Attribute	What's Changed
a	name	Use the id attribute instead.
img	border	The value must be set to '0' if used. Use CSS instead.
script	language	The value must be set to 'JavaScript' (case-insensitive) if used, and it cannot conflict with the type attribute. The value can be omitted because it has no use: there is only one language, JavaScript, that can be used with the script element.
table	summary	The HTML5 draft recommendation defines several alternative solutions.

Which attributes have been removed?

Some attributes from HTML4 are no longer allowed in HTML5. Many of them were deprecated in HTML4, but were still allowed.

Element	Attribute	Alternative (CSS unless specified)
a	coords	Use the area element
	name	Use the ID attribute
	shape	Use the area element
body	alink	a:active pseudo class
	background	background properties
	bgcolor	background-color property
	link	a:link pseudo class
	text	font-color property
	vlink	a:visited pseudo class
caption	align	text-align property
col	align	text-align property
	valign	vertical-align property
	width	width property
colgroup	align	text-align property
	valign	vertical-align property
	width	width property
div	align	text-align property
dl	compact	line-height property
embed	name	Use the ID attribute
h1-h6	align	text-align property
hr	align	margin properties
	noshade	border properties
	size	height property
	valign	vertical-align property
	width	width property
html	version	Not needed in HTML5
iframe	align	float property
	frameborder	border properties

Element	Attribute	Alternative (CSS unless specified)
	marginheight	margin properties in contained document
	marginwidth	margin properties in contained document
	scrolling	overflow property
img	align	float property
	hspace	margin properties
	name	Use the ID attribute
	vspace	margin properties
input	align	margin properties
legend	align	margin properties
li	type	list-style-type property
meta	scheme	Use the charset attribute
menu	compact	line-height property
object	align	margin properties
	archive	Use the data and type attributes
	border	border properties
	classid	Use the data and type attributes
	codebase	Use the data and type attributes
	codetype	Use the data and type attributes
	declare	Repeat the object element.
	hspace	margin properties
	standby	No alternative: "Optimize the linked resource so that it loads quickly."
	vspace	margin properties
ol	compact	line-height property
	type	list-style-type property
option	name	Use the ID attribute
pre	width	width property
	valign	vertical-align property
table	align	text-align property
	bgcolor	background-color property
	border	border properties
	cellpadding	padding property

Element	Attribute	Alternative (CSS unless specified)
	cellspacing	border-spacing property
	rules	border properties
	valign	vertical-align property
	width	width property
tbody	align	text-align property
td	align	text-align property
	axis	Use the scope attribute on the th tag
	bgcolor	background-color property
	height	line-height property
	nowrap	white-space:nowrap
	valign	vertical-align property
	width	width property
tfoot	align	text-align property
th	align	text-align property
	axis	Use the scope attribute
	bgcolor	background-color property
	height	line-height property
	nowrap	white-space:nowrap
	valign	vertical-align property
	width	width property
thead	align	text-align property
tr	align	text-align property
ul	compact	line-height property
	type	list-style-type property

What are the new window events?

The following window events are new in HTML5:

Event	When It Runs
onafterprint	After the document is printed.
onbeforeprint	Before the document is printed.
onbeforeonload	Before the document loads.
onerror	When there is a runtime scripting error.
onhashchange	When the hash component (i.e., the part after the # sign) of the URL changes.
onmessage	When a message is triggered.
onoffline	When a document goes offline.
ononline	When a document comes online.
onpagehide	When the window is hidden.
onpageshow	When the window becomes visible.
onpopstate	When the window's history changes.
onredo	When the user selects to redo a drag action.
onresize	When the window is resized.
onstorage	When the document loads.
onundo	When the user selects to undo a drag action.
onunload	When the document is closed.

What are the new mouse events?

The following mouse events are new in HTML5:

Event	When It Runs
ondrag	When an element is dragged.
ondragend	At the end of a drag action.
ondragenter	When an element is dragged to a valid drop target.
ondragleave	When an element is dragged out of a valid drop target.
ondragover	When an element is dragged over a valid drop target.
ondragstart	At the start of a drag action.
ondrop	When the element is dropped.
onmousewheel	When the mouse wheel is rotated.
onscroll	When an element's scrollbar is scrolled.

What are the new form events?

The following form elements are new in HTML5:

Event	When It Runs
oncontextmenu	When a context menu is triggered (usually by clicking the right mouse button).
onformchange	When the value of any element in a form changes.
onforminput	When any element's value in a form changes from the default.
oninput	When a form element's value changes from the default.
oninvalid	When a form element's value is invalid or when a required element's value is empty.

What are the new media events?

HTML5 adds the following media events. These events can be used for any element, but they are most often used with the audio, video, img, embed, and object elements.

Event	When It Runs
oncanplay	When the media can play but cannot completely play to the end without stopping to buffer.
oncanplaythrough	When the media can play to the end without buffering.
ondurationchange	If the media's length changes.
onemptied	If the media's source becomes "empty" due to a network problem or another error.
onended	When the media has finished playing.
onerror	If an error occurs while loading the element.
onloadeddata	When the element's data is loaded.
onloadedmetadata	When the duration and other media data is loaded.
onloadstart	When the browser starts to load the media data.
onpause	When the media data is paused.
onplay	When the media is about to start playing.
onplaying	When the media starts playing.
onprogress	When the browser is accessing the media data.
onratechange	If the media data's playing rate changes.
onreadystatechange	If the media's ready state changes.
onseeked	If the media's seeking attribute is no longer true and the seeking has ended.
onseeking	If the media's seeking attribute is true and the seeking has begun.
onstalled	If there is an error fetching the media data.
onsuspend	If the media data was not completely fetched.

Event	When It Runs
ontimeupdate	When the media changes its playing position.
onvolumechange	When the media changes the volume or if the volume is set to "mute."
onwaiting	When the media has stopped playing but is expected to resume.

What are the unsupported form events?

The following form event is not supported in HTML5:

Event	When It Runs
onreset	Runs when a form is reset.

Structure

How is an HTML5 document structured?

HTML5 documents can be structured using the following elements:

Element	Sample Content
header	A logo and/or page title
nav	Site-wide links
section	A collection of news articles
article	A blog post or news article
aside	Links to recent and popular articles
footer	A copyright statement

For example, a document may use the following structure:

What is a section?

The section element is used for self-contained blocks of content that typically have a heading. For example, a section could be a chapter, a tab in a tabbed dialog box, or a numbered section in a technical specification. The section element is not a generic container element. When an element is only needed for formatting or scripting, you should use a div element instead of a section.

◇ *The article element should be used instead of the section element if the content will be syndicated.*

Heading levels in sections are automatically adjusted to match the section's level. For example, an h1 in a nested section would become an h2.

Example

```
<section>
 <h1>Thomas Müller</h1>
 <p>German midfielder who received the Golden Boot award in the 2010 World
Cup.</p>
</section>
```

In the following example, the nested "Thomas Müller" h1 would become an h2:

```
<section>
 <h1>Germany</h1>
 <section>
  <h1>Thomas Müller</h1>
  <p>German midfielder who received the Golden Boot award in the 2010 World
Cup.</p>
 </section>
</section>
```

What is an article?

The article element is used for self-contained blocks of content that might be independently distributed. For example, an article element might contain a forum post, a news article, a blog entry, or a comment.

You can nest article elements, if needed. For example, a blog entry might be formatted as an article with nested articles for each comment.

Example

This example uses an article element for a blog post:

```
<article>
 <header>
  <h1>World Team of the 20th Century</h1>
 </header>
 <p>In 1998, 250 journalists selected an all-star team of the century. The team was composed of Yashin, Torres, Beckenbauer, Moore, Santos, Cruijff, Di Stéfano, Platini, Garrincha, Maradona, and Pelé.</p>
 <p>What's your opinion? Who should be the substitutes?</p>
 <footer>
  <a href="?comments=1">Show comments...</a>
 </footer>
</article>
```

What is the difference between a section and an article?

Sections and articles are very similar, and either one can be nested inside the other. The big difference is that an article can make sense if read by itself.

To Create...	Use This Element...
tabs on a page	section The tabs would not make sense if read by themselves.
blog post	article A blog post could be read by itself.
comments in a blog post	section The comments would not be read by themselves without the blog post.

What is a header?

The header element can be used to contain a document or section's heading, a section's table of contents, a search form, or a logo. The header element is not required, and it does not have to appear at the top of the document (or section) when presented or in the code.

The header element is not considered a sectioning element.

Example

In the following example, the document has a header, and each section within the document has its own header.

```
<header>
  <h1>World Cup Trivia</h1>
</header>
<p>This document provides interesting trivia about the World Cup.</p>
<section>
  <header>
    <h1>1954 World Cup Trivia</h1>
  </header>
  <p>...</p>
</section>
<section>
  <header>1994 World Cup Trivia</header>
  <p>...</p>
</section>
```

What is an hgroup?

The hgroup element represents a section's heading. It can be used to group a heading with subheadings, an alternative title, and/or a tagline.

For document summaries and outlines, the text of an hgroup element is set to the highest-ranked h1-h6 element. If there are multiple elements with the same rank, the first element is used. If there are no heading elements, the text of the hgroup element is an empty string.

The rank an hgroup element is the rank of the highest-ranked h1-h6 element within the hgroup.

Examples

In this example, the text of the hgroup would be set to 'World Cup Trivia' and the rank would be set to 1.

```
<section>
  <header>
   <hgroup>
     <h1>World Cup Trivia</h1>
     <h2>1954 World Cup Trivia</h2>
  </header>
  <p>...</p>
</section>
```

What is the difference between a header and an hgroup?

A header can contain any elements (except another header), but an hgroup can only contain a group of h1 through h6 elements. Since a header often contains h1-h6 elements, you will often have an hgroup inside of a header.

The purpose of the header is to contain a document or section's introductory and navigational content. The purpose of the hgroup is to only include the highest-level heading from the hgroup in the document's outline.

Example

```
<section>
  <header>
   <hgroup>
     <h1>World Cup Trivia</h1>
     <h2>1954 World Cup Trivia</h2>
<p><time datetime="2010-07-11">11th July, 2010</time></p
  </header>
</section>
```

How can I determine heading levels in complex documents?

You can use an outliner to view a document's heading structure. Since heading levels can automatically change based on how they are nested, an outliner can be very useful for documents with nested headings.

Check out the HTML5 Outliner at gsnedders.html5.org/outliner.

What is a footer?

The footer element can be used to contain a document or section's author's name, links to related documents, or a copyright statement. A footer can contain a section element to present an appendix or a long colophon or license agreement.

The footer element is not required, and it does not have to appear at the bottom of the document (or section) when presented or in the code.

The footer element is not considered a sectioning element.

Example

```
<header><h1>World Cup Trivia</h1></header>
<p>This document provides interesting trivia about the World Cup.</p>
<section>...</section>
<footer><p>Copyright 2010, ClickStart, Inc.</p></footer>
```

Can a document contain multiple headers or footers?

Yes.

You can use one header and footer for the entire document and separate headers and footers for each section within the document. However, headers and footers are not required for a document or section.

Example

In the following example, the document has a footer, and a section within the document has its own footer.

```
<header><h1>World Cup Trivia</h1></header>
<p>This document provides interesting trivia about the World Cup.</p>
<section>
  <header><h1>1954 World Cup Trivia</h1></header>
  <p>The highest scoring game was played in 1954: Austria 7, Switzerland 5.</p>
  <footer><p>Posted by Scott DeLoach</p></footer>
</section>
<footer><p>Copyright 2010, ClickStart, Inc.</p></footer>
```

What is the nav element?

The nav element should be used for a document's primary navigation links. A page can have multiple nav elements, but not all groups of links on a page need to be inside a nav element.

User agents such as screen readers can use nav elements either to omit the links in the initial rendering or to make them immediately available.

Example

In the following example, a nav element contains a document's menu.

```
<nav>
  <ul>
    <li><a href="home.htm">Home</a></li>
    <li><a href="posts.htm">Posts</a></li>
    <li><a href="about.htm">About us</a></li>
  </ul>
</nav>
```

What is an aside?

The aside element is used to present information that is related to the content surrounding it (such as a list of related links or pull quote) or content that is related to the site as a whole (such as a sidebar).

Example - Using aside as a pull quote

If you are using an aside to present a pull quote, it should be nested in an article element:

```
<article>
 <p>Franz Beckenbauer, nicknamed "Der Kaiser" is considered one the greatest soccer players in the history of the game. He is the only person to win the World Cup as both team captain and coach.</p>
 <aside>
 <p>It is not the strong one that wins. The one that wins is strong. ~ Franz Beckenbauer</p>
 </aside>
</article>
```

Example - Using aside as a sidebar

If you are using an aside to present information that relates to the site as a whole, it should not be nested in an article element:

```
<aside>
<h2>Recent posts</h2>
<p><a href="#">Match review: Germany 4, Australia 0</a></p>
<p><a href="#">Match review: Germany 4, England 1</a></p>
<p><a href="#">Match review: German 4, Argentina 0</a></p>
</aside>
```

What is the figure element?

The figure element can be used to annotate content that is referred to from the main content but could be moved to the side of the page. Some examples are illustrations, charts, diagrams, photos, multimedia, tables, and code listings.

The first figcaption element within a figure element is used as the figure's caption. If the figure element does not contain a figcaption element, it will not have a caption.

Example

The following example uses the figure element for an image:

```
<figure id="wc2010ball">
  <figcaption>World Cup 2010 Jabulani ball</figcaption>
  <img src="wc2010ball.png" />
</figure>
```

Does HTML5 use div elements?

Yes, you can use div elements in HTML5.

A div can be used to group content, such as a block of content you want to show and hide using a script. However, you shouldn't use a div if another element such as section or article is more appropriate.

What is the difference between an aside, figure, and div element?

The aside, figure, and div elements are similar, but there are basic differences between them:

- If the content is related to the main content but it is not essential information, use the aside element.

- If the content is essential but its position isn't important, use the figure element.

- If the position is important, use a div, img, or possibly canvas element.

What is the address element?

The address element is used to format the contact information for the author of a section, article, or document. It should only be used for the author's contacct information, not all addresses in a document. It is typically used for email or webpage links rather than postal addresses.

Example

```
<address>
This document was written by:<br>
<a href=mailto:scott@clickstart.net">Scott DeLoach</a>
</address>
```

Format

Does HTML5 use classes?

Yes, and you can now access them using the new classList method. See "How do I find all of the elements that use a specified style class?" on page 52.

Is there an HTML5 "reset" stylesheet?

Yes.

A "reset" stylesheet sets all elements to a generic baseline to prevent different browser defaults from causing inconsistencies. You should definitely use a reset stylesheet if you are developing HTML5 for older browsers. Otherwise, the browser will not know how to display the new elements.

Remy Sharp has posted a free HTML5 reset stylesheet to the HTML5 Doctor site at www.html5doctor.com/html-5-reset-stylesheet.

Can I format the new HTML5 elements using CSS?

Yes.

The new elements can be formatted as follows:

```
header { CSS style definitions }
nav { CSS style definitions }
section { CSS style definitions }
article { CSS style definitions }
aside  { CSS style definitions }
footer { CSS style definitions }
```

How do I define styles for part of a document?

You can use the scoped attribute to define styles for part of a document rather than the entire document.

Example

```
<article>
<style scoped>
  h1 { color:#ff0000 }
</style>
<h1>Berlin</h1>
</article>
```

How do I find all of the elements that use a specified style class?

You can use the getElementsByClassName() method to create a live NodeList object that contains all of the elements, in DOM tree order, whose class attribute is set to a specified class. If a class is not specified, the getElementsByClassName() method will contain an empty NodeList object.

◇ If the document is in quirks mode (see page 14), the class name string is not case sensitive.

Example

This script will display an alert dialog box that contains the text "Hi there!"

```
<p class="example" id="sample">Hi there!</p>
<script>
var myNodes = document.getElementsByClassName('example');
alert(myNodes[0].innerHTML);
</script>
```

How do I modify an element's style class?

You can use the classList attribute to:

- Determine whether an element's class name contains a string

- Add a class to an element

- Remove a class from an element

- Toggle an element's class name

Method	Definition
add('classname')	Sets an element's style class.
contains('classname')	Returns true if the element is assigned the specified class name.
remove('classname')	Removes the specified class name from the element.
toggle('classname')	Alternates between adding and removing the specified class name from the element.

The relList attribute provides similar information for the a, area, and link elements.

How do I emphasize important content?

You can use the mark element to emphasize content in a quote that was not emphasized by the original author or to emphasize content that you think is important.

Example

```
<p>Practice makes <mark>permanent</mark>.</p>
```

What is the difference between the mark and strong elements?

The mark element's name does not imply a specific format, such as bold. It can be used to italicize, boldface, or highlight content. For example, the mark element might be used to highlight search terms in a document. The strong element is best used to indicate important content, such as a warning.

How do I specify a line break?

You can use the br element to specify a line break, or you can use the wbr element to specify a potential break within a long word or text string without spaces.

Example - br element

```
<p>The Local<br>
758 Ponce De Leon Ave NE<br>
Atlanta, GA 30306</p>
```

Example - wbr element

```
Hippopoto<wbr>monstro<wbr>sesquipedalian
```

How do I create a datagrid?

You can use a datagrid to display data as a tree, list, or table. The data can stored in the datagrid, or it can be provided by a script.

The rows in a datagrid are numbered starting with 0, and each row can have its own child rows. The child rows can be hidden or displayed by closing or opening the parent row. A datagrid can have multiple columns, and each column can have a caption.

 The datagrid element may be removed from HTML5.

Attribute	Description
disabled	Specifies whether the datagrid is disabled.
multiple	Specifies whether the user can select multiple rows at the same time.

Example

```
<datagrid disabled>
 <ol>
  <li>row 0</li>
  <li>row 1
   <ol style="list-style-type:lower-alpha;">
    <li>row 1.0</li>
    <li>row 1.1</li>
   </ol>
  </li>
  <li>row 2</li>
 </ol>
</datagrid>
```

How do I create a definition list?

You can use the dl element with the dt, dfn, and dd elements to create a definition list for a glossary.

Example

```
<dl>
 <dt><dfn>Bundesliga</dfn></dt>
  <dd>The premier soccer league in Germany.</dd>
 <dt><dfn>Die Mannschaft</dfn></dt>
  <dd>The German national soccer team.</dd>
</dl>
```

How do I specify the date and time?

You can use the time element to specify a date and time in a document. Content in a time element could then be used in search engine rankings or added to the user's calendar.

The date must be a positive date using the Gregorian calendar, and it must include a day, month, and year.

Attribute	Description
pubdate	Specifies that the date and time should be used as the publication date and time of the parent article element. If the time element does not have a parent article element, the pubdate is applied to the entire document.

Example

```
<time datetime="2010-10-15">October 15 2010</time>
<time datetime="2009-10-15">October 15<sup>th</sup></time>
<time datetime="2010-10-15T012:00Z">10/15 at 12pm</time>
<time datetime="2010-10-15" pubdate>Input element browser support
```

How do I use the dialog element?

You can use the dialog element to indicate a conversation. The dt element should be used to indicate the speaker, and the dd element should be used to indicate the quote.

 The dialog element may be removed from HTML5.

Example

```
<dialog>
<dt>Boris</dt>
<dd>I've made up my mind. I'm going away.</dd>
<dt>Domini</dt>
<dd>Then I shall be alone.</dd>
<dt>Boris</dt>
<dd>That journey into the desert you've spoken of. You will take it alone?</dd>
<dt>Domini</dt>
<dd>What else can I do?</dd>
<dt>Boris</dt>
<dd>Once, you said to me that peace and happiness might be found there. You gave me
hope, and now....Now, we have to say goodbye.</dd>
<dt>Domini</dt>
<dd>Goodbye.</dd>
</dialog>
```

How do I create a numbered list in reversed order?

You can use the ol element's "reversed" attribute to create a numbered list in reverse (i.e., 3, 2, 1) order.

This attribute is not currently supported in any browser, but it should be supported in the future.

Example

```
<ol reversed="reversed">
 <li>Oliver Bierhoff</li>
 <li>Oliver Kahn</li>
 <li>Michael Ballack</li>
</ol>
```

Forms

How do I add placeholder text to a field?

You can use the input element's 'placeholder' attribute to add placeholder text to an input element. Placeholder text disappears when an input element has focus.

Example

```
<input name="sample" placeholder="Sample text">
```

```
Sample text
```

How do I automatically give focus to an input element?

You can use the autofocus attribute to automatically give focus to an input element.

Example

```
<input name="sample" autofocus>
```

TIP *If your browser does not support the autofocus attribute, you can use JavaScript to give focus to an input element:*

```
<input id="sample" autofocus>
<script>
if (!("autofocus" in document.createElement("input")))
{ document.getElementById("sample").focus(); }
</script>
```

How do I create an email input element?

You can use the input element's 'email' type to create an email address text box. The email text box will display a message if the email address is not valid.

Example

<input name="myEmail" type="email">

How do I create a URL text box?

You can use the input element's 'URL' type to create a URL text box. The URL text box will display a message if the URL is not valid.

Example

<input name="myURL" type="url">

How do I create a range input element?

You can use the input element's 'range' type to allow the user to graphically select a number using a slider. The range type is a less precise alternative to the number type.

Attribute	Description
step	The amount that is added or subtracted when the slider is moved.
max	The maximum allowed value. The default is 100.
min	The minimum allowed value. The default is 0.
value	The initial value. The default is the average of the min and max.

Example

<input name="vol" type="range" min="1" max="11" value="7" step="1">

How do I create a number input element?

You can use the input element's 'number' type to allow the user to select or type a number.

Attribute	Description
step	The amount that is added or subtracted when the slider is moved. For example, a range element with a min of 1, a max of 10, and a step of 2 would allow five numbers to be selected (1, 3, 5, 7, and 9).
max	The maximum allowed value. The default is 100.
min	The minimum allowed value. The default is 0.
value	The initial value.

Example

<input name="myNum" type="number" min="0" max="10" step="1" value="2">

How do I create a time selector?

You can set the input element's 'time' type to create a time selector.

Example

<input name="myTime" type="time">

How do I create a date selector?

You can use the input element's 'date' type to create a date, date and time, week, or month selector.

Examples

<input name="myDate" type="date">

<input name="myDateTime" type="datetime">

<input name="myWeek" type="week">

```
<input name="myMonth" type="month">
```

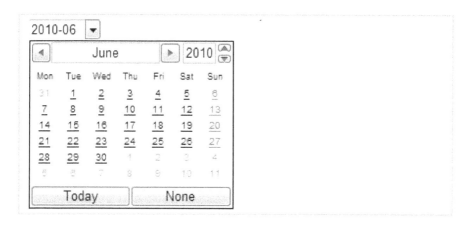

How do I create a color selector?

You can use the input element's 'color' type to create an RGB (red, green, blue) color selector.

Example

```
<input name="myColor" type="color">
```

How do I create a search field?

You can use the input element's 'search' type to create a search field.

Example

```
<input name="mySearch" type="search">
```

How do I create a telephone number field?

You can use the input element's 'tel' type to create a telephone field. The tel type does not require numeric-only input, but you can use the pattern attribute to validate the user's input. The tel type may appear as a telephone keypad in some browsers, so it is a good alternative to the number type.

Example

```
<input name="myTel" type="tel">
```

How do I use the optgroup element?

The optgroup element can be used to group items in a drop-down listbox.

Attribute	Description
disabled	Specifies that the group cannot be selected.
label	Specifies the group's name. This value is required.

Example

```
<select>
  <optgroup label="Germany">
    <option value ="berlin">Berlin</option>
    <option value ="munich">Munich</option>
  </optgroup>
  <optgroup label="Russia">
    <option value ="moscow">Moscow</option>
    <option value ="petersburg">St Petersburg</option>
  </optgroup>
</select>
```

How do I provide an autocomplete option for a textbox?

You can use a datalist to add autocomplete options to an input element.

Attribute	Description
data	Specifies an XML file that can be used to prefill the datalist.

Example

```
<input list="players">
 <datalist id="players">
  <option value="Miroslav Klose">
  <option value="Bastian Schweinsteiger">
  <option value="Philipp Lahm">
  <option value="Mesut Oezil">
 </datalist>
```

How do I store and auto-fill a form element's value?

You can use the autocomplete attribute to store and auto-fill an input element when the user returns to the document.

Example

```
<input name="sample" autocomplete="on">
```

Can I use the input element's new types with older browsers?

Yes.

If a browser does not recognize an input element's type, it will use the 'text' type.

TIP▶ *Many of the new types already work on the iPhone and other mobile devices.*

How do I associate an element with a form?

If an element (such as an input element) is contained in a form element, it is automatically associated with the form element. However, you can use the form attribute to associate an element with a form if it is outside the form element.

Example

```
<form id=feedback></form>
<input type="text" form=feedback>
```

How do I require the user to provide a value?

You can use the required attribute to require the user to provide a value before submitting the form. The browser will identify any blank required form elements. For example, Safari highlights the form element's border.

Example

```
<label>First name
<input name="fname" required>
</label>
```

```
11
```
11 is not in the
format this page
requires!
A social security number
has nine digits.

How do I verify a form element's value?

You can use the pattern attribute to specify a regular expression that will be used to verify an element's value.

Example

```
<label>SSN:
<input pattern="[0-9]{9}" name="ssn" title="A social security number has nine digits." >
</label>
```

```
11
```
11 is not in the
format this page
requires!
A social security number
has nine digits.

Can I enable spellchecking for form elements or editable content?

Yes. You can use the spellcheck attribute to spellcheck user-provided content.

 The spellcheck attribute can be written as spellcheck="true" or simply as spellcheck.

Example

<p spellcheck="true" contenteditable="true">type your favorite city here</p>
City: <input type="text" spellcheck="true" >

Rejkjavik

City: Rekjavik

How do I use the keygen element?

You can use the keygen element to generate a public-private key pair and to submit the public key.

Attribute	Description
challenge	Specifies that the value should be challenged when submitted.
keytype	Defines the keytype, such as rsa.

Example

```
<form>
  <p>Username: <input type="text" name="username" ></p>
  <p>Encryption: <keygen name="security" challenge ></p>
  <input type="submit" >
</form>
```

Username:

Encryption: 1024 (Medium Grade) ▼

Submit 2048 (High Grade)
        1024 (Medium Grade)

Images, Videos, and Sounds

Does HTML5 support SVG?

Yes.

SVG stands for 'Scalable Vector Graphics.' SVG images are based on XML, and they offer the following advantages:

- They don't lose quality when they are zoomed or resized.

- They are smaller than GIF and JPG images.

- Text in SVG images can be selected and searched.

The SVG format includes the following elements:

Element	What It Does	Attributes
circle	Creates a circle.	cx and cy - the x and y coordinates of the center of the circle. If cx and cy are omitted, the circle's center is set to 0, 0. r - the radius of the circle fill – the color to use to fill the circle
ellipse	Creates an ellipse (i.e., an oval).	cx - the x coordinate of the ellipse's center cy -the y coordinate of the ellipse's center rx - the horizontal radius ry - the vertical radius fill – the fill color
line	Creates a line.	x1 - the start of the line on the x-axis y1 - the start of the line on the y-axis x2 - the end of the line on the x-axis y2 - the end of the line on the y-axis
path	Creates a shape that consists of curved lines.	M - moveto L - lineto

Element	What It Does	Attributes
		H - horizontal lineto
		V - vertical lineto
		C - curveto
		S - smooth curveto
		Q - quadratic Bézier curve
		T - smooth quadratic Bézier curveto
		A - elliptical Arc
		Z - closepath
		All of the commands above can be expressed with uppercase or lowercase letters. Uppercase means absolute positioning, and lowercase means relative positioning.
polygon	Creates a shape with at least three sides.	points - the x and y coordinates for each corner
polyline	Creates a shape that consists of straight lines.	points - the x and y coordinates for each corner
rect	Creates a rectangle.	height – the height of the rectangle
		width – the width of the rectangle
		x – the starting x coordinate for the left top corner
		y – the starting y coordinate for the left top corner
		rx - the horizontal corner curve radius
		ry - the vertical corner curve radius

Circle

The following example creates a red circle:

```
<svg><circle r="50" cx="50" cy="50" fill="green" stroke="#00cc00" /></svg>
```

Ellipse

The following example creates a green ellipse:

```
<svg><ellipse cx="40" cy="40" rx="30" ry="15" fill="#00ff00" stroke="#00ff00" /></svg>
```

Line

The following example creates a green line:

```
<svg><line x1="0" y1="10" x2="0" y2="100" fill="#00ff00" stroke="#00ff00" /></svg>
```

Path

The following example creates a green "U" shape:

```
<svg><path d="M80,20 A20,50 0 1,0 150,20" stroke="#00ff00" fill="none" /></svg>
```

Polygon

The following example creates a green octagon:

```
<svg><polygon points="25,0 65,0 90,20 90,65 65,90 25,90 0,65 0,25" stroke="#00ff00" fill="#00ff00" /></svg>
```

Polyline

The following example creates a green triangle:

```
<svg><polyline points="0,0 30,0 15,30" fill="#00ff00" stroke="#00ff00" /></svg>
```

Rectangle

The following example creates a green rectangle with rounded corners:

```
<svg><rect x="0" y="0" height="50" width="50" rx="15" ry="15" fill="#00ff00" stroke="#00ff00" /></svg>
```

How do I use the canvas element?

You can use the canvas element to create a drawing area (the "canvas"). After you create a canvas, you can draw graphics inside the canvas using JavaScript.

You can write scripts to draw graphics inside a canvas element, but you should use an application to draw anything more than basic shapes. For example, you can use Flash CS5 to create complex and animated graphics for a canvas element using JavaScript.

Attribute	Description
height	Sets the height of the canvas element in pixels.
width	Sets the width of the canvas element in pixels.

TIP▷ *See www.canvasdemos.com for examples and development tools.*

The following table explains the functions that can be used to draw basic shapes.

Shape	Functions	Description
arcs	arc(x, y, radius, startAngle, endAngle, anticlockwise)	startAngle – the start point of the arc (in radians)
		endAngle – the end point of the arc (in radians)
		anticlockwise – Boolean value to draw the arc anticlockwise
		TIP▷ *You can use the following expression to convert degrees to radians:* *var radians = degrees * (Math.PI/180)*
curves – Bézier	bezierCurveTo(cp1x, cp1y, cp2x, cp2y, x, y)	cp1x – the x coordinate of the first control point
		cp1y – the y coordinate of the first control point
		cp2x – the x coordinate of the second control point
		cp2y – the y coordinate of the second control point
curves – quadratic	quadraticCurveTo(cp1x, cp1y, x, y)	cp1x – the x coordinate of the first control point
		cp1y – the y coordinate of the first control point
lines / paths	beginPath() closePath() fill() lineTo(x,y)	Starts a new shape Draws a line to the start point of the first path Fills the shape Draws a line starting at the

Shape	Functions	Description
	moveTo(x,y)	previous point
	stroke()	Starts a new line
		Draws an outline shape
rectangles	fillRect(x,y,width,height);	Draws a filled rectangle
	strokeRect(x,y,width,height);	Draws a rectangular outline
	clearRect(x,y,width,height);	Makes the specified area transparent
rectangles	rect(x, y, width, height)	x and y - the top left corner's location

The canvas element can also be used to insert, slice, and scale an image. It also supports numerous methods. For a full tutorial on using all of the available methods, see developer.mozilla.org/en/Canvas_tutorial.

Example - specifying alternate text

```
<canvas id="barchart" width="300" height="300">Sales are up 10% this quarter</canvas>
```

Example - specifying an alternate image

```
<canvas id="barchart" width="300" height="300">
  <img src="barchart.png" width="300" height="300" />
</canvas>
```

Example - drawing a rectangle

```
<script>
function draw() {
  var canvas = document.getElementById('myShape');
  if (canvas.getContext) {
    var drw = canvas.getContext('2d');
    drw.fillStyle = "rgb(0,100,0)";
    drw.fillRect(10,10,100,50);
} }
</script>
<canvas id="myShape" width="300" height="300">A green rectangle</canvas>
```

Should I use SVG or canvas elements?

SVG and canvas elements can both be used to create graphics. The biggest difference is that the SVG element is vector-based and the canvas element is raster-based. The following table compares SVG and canvas elements based on other common criteria:

Criteria	canvas	SVG
Accessibility		✓
Animation		✓
Element-level control using DOM		✓
Pixel-level manipulation	✓	
Scalability		✓
Speed	✓	
Rendering text		✓
UI design – applications		✓
UI design - games*		

* Since games require pixel-level manipulation (a strength of canvas) and interactivity (a strength of SVG), the best approach is a combination of both elements.

How do I include audio files?

You can use the audio element to add audio to a document. It includes the following attributes:

Attribute	Description
autoplay	Starts loading the audio immediately when the page loads and plays the audio as soon as it's buffered.
controls	Adds playback controls.
loop	Replays the audio when it is finished playing.
preload	Starts loading the audio immediately on page load, but does not play the audio.

Attribute	Description
src	Specifies the URL of the audio file.

Example

<audio src="deutschlandlied.oga" type="audio/ogg"></audio>

How do I support different browsers?

Unfortunately, no audio format is natively supported by all of the major browsers. However, you can use the source element to specify alternate audio files. The browser can then select a format based on its media type or codec support.

◇ *When you use the source element, the audio element's src attribute should be omitted. Otherwise, the source element will be ignored.*

The following table summarizes the audio formats that are supported by the current versions of popular browsers:

Format	IE	Firefox	Chrome	Safari	Opera
aac	✓	✓	✓	✓	
mp3	✓		✓	✓	
ogg		✓	✓		✓
wav		✓		✓	✓
webm		✓	✓		✓

TIP▷ *To test your browser's support for various audio formats, see www.html5test.com.*

Example

<audio>
  <source src="deutschlandlied.oga" type="audio/ogg">
  <source src="deutschlandlied.mp3" type="audio/mpeg">
</audio>

How do I include video files?

You can use the video element to add video to a document. It includes the following attributes:

Attribute	Description
autoplay	Starts loading the video immediately on page load and plays it when it is loaded.
controls	Adds playback controls.
height	Sets the video's height.
loop	Replays the video when it is finished playing.
preload	Starts loading the video immediately on page load, but does not play the video.
src	Specifies the URL of the video file.
width	Sets the video's width.

If you only specify the width or height, the video will be sized to preserve its aspect ratio. If you specify a width and height that does not match the video's aspect ratio, the video will be letter-boxed using its original aspect ratio.

Example

```
<video src="myvideo.mp4" type="video/mp4" autoplay></video>
```

How do I specify multiple videos?

Different browsers support different video formats. For example, Chrome, Firefox, and Opera support the ogg format, and Safari and the iPhone/iPad support mp4. The source element can be used to specify alternative video files to allow the browser to select a supported format.

When you use the source element, the video element's src attribute should be omitted. Otherwise, the source element will be ignored.

The following table summarizes video format support in popular browsers:

Format	IE	Firefox	Chrome	Safari	Opera
mp4 (h.264)	✓			✓	
ogg		✓	✓		✓
webm		✓	✓		✓

TIP▶ *To test your browser's support for various video formats, see www.html5test.com.*

Attribute	Description
src	Specifies the URL of the video file.
type	Specifies the video's type and (optionally) the codec.

Example

```
<video>
 <source src="myvideo.mp4" type="video/mp4">
 <source src="myvideo.ogg" type="video/ogg">
</video>
```

How do I specify smaller videos for handheld devices?

You can use the media attribute to specify videos based on the browsing device's size. Current handheld device screens are smaller than 800px, so you can specify larger videos for screens that are larger than 800px.

Example

```
<video>
 <source src="myvideo_small.mp4" type="video/mp4">
 <source src="myvideo_full.mp4" type="video/mp4" media="min-device-width: 800px">
</video>
```

How do I include SWFs or FLV files in HTML5 documents?

You can use the object element to include SWF or FLV files.

Example

In this example, the object element is placed inside the video element. Browsers that support the video element will open the mp4 file, and browsers that do not support the video element will open the object element's swf file.

```
<video>
  <source src="myvideo.mp4" type="video/mp4">
  <object data="myvideo.swf" type="application/x-shockwave-flash">
   <param value="myvideo.swf" name="movie" />
  </object>
</video>
```

How do I set a video's 'picture'?

You can use the poster attribute to set the image that appears before the video is played.

```
<video src="myvideo.mp4" type="video/mp4" poster="startpix.jpg"></video>
```

How do I support older browsers?

You can include a download link to allow users with browsers that do not support the video element to download the video. Or, you can use the object element to allow older browsers to play the video.

Example: providing a download link

```
<video>
  <source src="myvideo.mp4" type="video/mp4">
  <a href="myvideo.mp4">Download the video</a>.
</video>
```

Example: using the object element

```
<video>
  <source src="myvideo.mp4" type="video/mp4">
  <object data="myvideo.swf" type="application/x-shockwave-flash">
    <param value="myvideo.swf" name="movie" />
  </object>
</video>
```

How do I autoplay a video?

You can use the autoplay attribute to autoplay a video:

```
<video src="myvideo.mp4" type="video/mp4" autoplay></video>
```

How do I preload a video?

You can use the preload attribute to preload a video so that it is ready when the user clicks the "play" control button. The preload attribute has three states:

State	Description
auto	Requests that the browser should begin downloading the file. However, the browser may be configured to ignore the request.
none	The video is not downloaded until the video plays.
metadata	The video's metadata (e.g., the dimensions and duration) is downloaded but not the video itself.

Example

```
<video src="myvideo.mp4" type="video/mp4" control preload="auto"></video>
```

How do I loop a video?

You can use the loop attribute to continuously replay a video.

```
<video src="myvideo.mp4" type="video/mp4" loop></video>
```

How do I add playback controls to a video?

You can use the control attribute to add playback control buttons to a video, such as play, pause, rewind, and fast forward.

Example

```
<video width="600" height="300" src="myvideo.mp4" type="video/mp4" controls>
```

How do I match subtitles to a video?

Yes.

Subtitles are not currently part of the HTML5 recommendation, but you can use JavaScript to match a subtitle document (i.e., an srt file) to an HTML5 video. Jan Gerber has written a jQuery-based script to match an srt file to a video. The JavaScript code is available at v2v.cc/~j/jquery.srt.

Example

The following example uses Gerber's script to link a video to an srt file:

```
<script type="text/javascript" src="jquery.js"></script>
<script type="text/javascript" src="jquery.srt.js"></script>
<video src="video.ogv" type="video/mp4" id="video" controls></video>
<div class="srt" data-video="video" data-srt="subtitles.srt" />
```

How do I resize a video?

You can use JavaScript and/or CSS to change a video element's width and/or height.

Example

The following CSS example changes a video's width on hover.

```
video:hover { width:800px; }
```

How do I control audio and video playback?

HTML5 provides an extensive API library with several methods and events that can be used to control media playback. The simplest methods are play(), pause(), and currentTime() (which can be used to rewind the media to the beginning).

Example

```
<video src="video.ogg" type="video/ogg" id="video"></video>
<script>
 var video = document.getElementById("video");
</script>
  <button type="button" onclick="video.play();">Play</button>
  <button type="button" onclick="video.pause();">Pause</button>
  <button type="button" onclick="video.currentTime = 0;">Rewind</button>
```

For more information about controlling playback, see www.w3.org/TR/html5.

How do I jump to a position in a video?

You can use JavaScript to jump to a specified location in a video.

Example

```
<video width="600" height="300" src="myvideo2.mp4" controls></video>
<p><a href="javascript:void()" onClick="jumpVideo()">jump</a></p>
<script>
function jumpVideo() {
 var video = document.getElementsByTagName("video")[0];
 video.currentTime = 100;
}
</script>
```

How do I use the device element to add video conferencing?

You can use the device element to access a device, such as a webcam.

Attribute	Description
type	Specifies the kind of device the element will access: media (audio or video), fs (file system), or rs232 (a serial port).

Example

```
<p>To start a chat session, click here: <device type=media
onchange="update(this.data)"></p>
<video autoplay></video>
<script>
function update(stream) { document.getElementsByTagName('video')[0].src = stream.url; }
</script>
```

How do I embed interactive content?

You can use the embed element to insert an application or interactive content.

Example

```
<embed type="video/quicktime" src="klose_goal.mov" width="400" height="400" />
```

Interactivity and Updating Content

How can I change a document or element's contents?

You can use the innerHTML() method to return or set a document or element's contents.

Example

This script will display an alert dialog box that contains the text "Hi there!"

```
<p id="sample">Hi there!</p>
<script>
alert(document.getElementById("sample").innerHTML);
</script>
```

How can I determine which element has focus?

You can use the activeElement attribute to find the element that currently has focus.

Example

```
var curElement = document.activeElement;
```

How do I determine if the document has focus?

You can use the hasFocus() method to determine if the document has focus.

Example

```
focused = document.hasFocus();
```

How do I determine the currently selected content?

You can use the getSelection() method to read the selected content in the document.

Example

```
var winSel = window.getSelection();
alert(winSel);
```

How do I use the details element?

The details element allows the user to show and hide content (the W3C calls it a 'disclosure widget'). It is collapsed (i.e., 'hidden') by default. Any content contained in a summary element inside the details element will appear as the details element's heading. If the details element does not contain a summary element, the default heading is 'Details.'

Example

```
<details>
  <summary>We are the music makers...</summary>
  <p>And we are the dreamers of dreams.</p>
</details>
```

Closed state

 We are the music makers...

Open state

 We are the music makers...
And we are the dreamers of dreams.

How do I use the eventsource element?

You can use the eventsource element to display information from an external source, such as a script or a web-based application.

Attribute	Description
src	The path and filename of the external resource that will provide the data. The resource must send the data using the text/event-stream format.

Example

<eventsource src="http://mysite.com" onmessage="alert(event.data)" >

How do I use the command element?

You can use the command element to define and reuse a command for a menu, button, or link.

Attribute	Description
checked	Specifies whether the command is selected (Boolean value).
default	For a context menu, this attribute specifies that the command should be invoked if the user selects the menu instead of a command in the menu.
disabled	Specifies whether the command is disabled (Boolean value).
icon	Specifies the URL of an image to display as the command.

Attribute	Description
label	Defines the command element's name. The label is visible.
radiogroup	If the type is set to radio, specifies the radiogroup the command belongs to.
title	Specifies a tooltip for the command.
type	Specifies the type of command: checkbox, command, or radio. The default is command.

Example

```
<menu type="popup" label="Help">
 <command onclick="helpTOC()" label=" TOC" >
 <command onclick="helpSearch()" label="Search" >
 <command onclick="about()" label="About" >
</menu>
```

How do I use the menu element?

The menu element can be used to create a toolbar, context menu, or list of commands.

Attribute	Description
label	Specifies the menu's label, which can be used to display nested menus.
type	Specifies the menu type: context, list (default), or toolbar.

Example

```
<p contextmenu="feedback">This paragraph has a context menu.</p>
<menu id="feedback">
 <command label="Add comment" onclick="comment();">
 <command label="Edit text" onclick="edit();">
 <command label="Delete" onclick="delete();">
</menu>
```

How do I use the output element?

You can use the output element to display the results of a calculation from a script or a value selected using a form element.

Attribute	Description
for	Creates a relationship between the result of a calculation and the elements that represent or influence the values that were used in the calculation. The value must be one or more element IDs (separated by a space) within the same document.
form	Specifies the associated form.
name	Specifies the output element's name.

Example

```
<form onsubmit="return false">
  <input name=aaa type=number step=any> +
  <input name=bbb type=number step=any> =
  <output onforminput="value = aaa + bbb "></output>
</form>
```

How do I use the meter element?

The meter element can be used to indicate an amount within a set range, such as a percentage.

✎ *You should only use the meter element if there is a known minimum and maximum value. To create an input element for values without a known minimum and maximum, use the 'number' type.*

Attribute	Description
high	The highest number of the meter's range. If the high is greater than the max, it is reset to the max value.
low	The lowest number of the meter's range. If the low is less than the min, it is reset to the min value.
max	The maximum allowed value. The default is 1.

Attribute	Description
min	The minimum allowed value. The default is 0.
optimum	The ideal value. The optimum must be between the min and max.
value	The current value.

Example

<meter value="50" max="100">50</meter>

How do I use the progress element?

The progress element can be used to indicate when an event will be completed. Its value can be updated with a script.

 To display a gauge, use the meter element.

Attribute	Description
max	The completed value.
value	The current progress value.

Example

<progress value="11" max="100">11%</progress>

11%

How do I specify the tab order of elements?

You can use the tabindex attribute to add any element to the tab list and to specify its position in the list.

 The tabindex values begin at 1.

Examples

```
<p tabindex="1">How many times has Germany won the World Cup?</p>
<input name="WCwins" type="text" tabindex="2">
```

Frames

Can I use frames?

HTML5 does not support frames because "their usage affected usability and accessibility for the end user in a negative way." You can still use frames, but your document will not be valid. Instead, you should use an iframe.

Can I use iframes?

Yes, you can use iframes in HTML5.

How do I make an iframe more secure?

You can use the sandbox attribute to make an iframe more secure.

Value	Description
allow-forms	Enables use of forms in an iframe's content.
allow-same-origin	Enables access to the DOM of the parent page.
allow-scripts	Enables use of scripts in an iframe's content, such as reading or writing cookies or local content (including SQL databases)/
allow-top-navigation	Enables elements in the iframe to change the URL of the containing document.

Example

<iframe src="example.htm" width="400" height="200" sandbox="allow-scripts allow-forms"></iframe>

Internationalization and Accessibility

How do I specify the character encoding for a document?

You can set a document's character encoding as follows:

- ▫ HTML syntax: <meta charset="utf-8">

- ▫ XHTML syntax: <?xml version="1.0" encoding="UTF-8" ?>

How do I specify the language for a document or element?

You can use the lang attribute to specify the language for a document or an element. The specified language could then be used by a text-to-speech converter or search engine.

For a list of lang attribute values, see www.iana.org/assignments/language-subtag-registry

Examples

```
<html lang="is">
<p lang="is">Hvað segir þú gott?</p>
```

Does HTML5 support IRIs?

Yes.

IRIs (International Resource Identifiers) can be used to specify a link location using Unicode, including Kanji, Arabic, Hebrew, and Cyrillic characters.

HTML5 has native support for IRIs, but they should only be used if the document encoding is UTF-8 or UTF-16.

Examples

卓球動画.com
президент.рф
مصر.الأتصــــــالات-وزارة

How do I add pronunciation guides?

You can use the ruby, rp, and rt elements to add pronunciation guides to content.

Element	Description
ruby	An inline element that contains a ruby annotation.
rt	The ruby text (i.e., the pronunciation annotations).
rp	Parentheses around the ruby text (rt). The rp tag is included so that the ruby text is enclosed in parentheses when displayed inline by non-supporting browsers: 京 - ruby-supporting browser 京 (きょう) – non-supporting browser

TIP▶ *'Ruby' was the British typographical name for type with a height of 5.5 pts. For a list of type names, see en.wikipedia.org/wiki/Point_ (typography)#Traditional_point-size_names.*

Examples

<p>Ferdinand <ruby>Porsche <rp>(</rp><rt>pɔːʃə</rt><rp>)</rp></ruby> also designed the original Volkswagen Beetle. </p>

Ferdinand Porsche also designed the original Volkswagen Beetle.

`<p><ruby>新幹線<rp>(</rp><rt>shinkansen</rt><rp>)</rp></ruby></p>`

新幹線
shinkansen

What is WAI-ARIA?

WAI-ARIA stands for "Web Accessibility Initiative – Accessible Rich Internet Applications." It provides a role attribute that can be used to make web content and applications more accessible.

The WAI-ARIA role attributes are:

Role Attribute	Description
banner	Content at the top of the document, such as an advertisement or company logo.
contentinfo	Information about the document's content such as footnotes, copyrights, and legal statements.
definition	A definition for a dfn element within the content.
main	The document's main content.
navigation	A collection of links that can be used to navigate the document or related documents.
note	Indicates that the content supports the main content.
search	The search section of the document.
secondary	A unique section of the document.
seealso	Indicates that the element contains content that is related to the page's main content.

How can I use WAI-ARIA with HTML5?

The following HTML5 elements have "strong native semantics" and therefore implied WAI-ARIA roles.

Element	Implied WAI-ARIA Role or State
any disabled element	aria-disabled state set to "true"
any required element	aria-required state set to "true"
a	link
area	link
button	button
datalist	listbox
h1-h6 (outside an hgroup)	heading, with aria-level property set to the element's outline depth
hgroup	heading, with aria-level property set to the element's outline depth
hr	separator
img	presentation
input - "button" type	button
input - "checkbox" type	checkbox, with aria-checked set to "mixed" if the element is not checked and "true" if the element is checked
input - "color" type	none
input - "date" date	none, with aria-readonly set to "true" if the element is readonly
input - "date and time" type	none, with aria-readonly set to "true" if the element is readonly
input - "local date and time" type	none, with aria-readonly set to "true" if the element is readonly
input - "e-mail" type	textbox, with aria-readonly set to "true" if the element is readonly
input - "file upload" type	button
input - "hidden" type	none
input - "image button" type	button

Element	Implied WAI-ARIA Role or State
input – "month" type	none, with aria-readonly set to "true" if the element is readonly
input – "number" type	spinbutton, with: □ aria-readonly set to "true" if the element is readonly □ aria-valuemax set to the element's maximum □ aria-valuemin set to the element's minimum □ aria-valuenow set to the element's value if it is a number
input – "password" type	textbox, with aria-readonly set to "true" if the element is readonly
input – "radio button" type	radio, with aria-checked set to "true" if the element is checked or "false" if it is not checked
input – "range" type	slider, with: □ aria-valuemax set to the element's maximum □ aria-valuemin set to the element's minimum □ aria-valuenow set to the element's value if it is a number
input – "reset button" type	button
input – "search" type	textbox, with aria-readonly set to "true" if the element is readonly
input – "submit button" type	button
input – "telephone" type	textbox, with aria-readonly set to "true" if the element is readonly
input – "text" type	textbox, with aria-readonly set to "true" if the element is readonly
input – type set to text, search, telephone, URL, or e-mail with a suggestions source element	combo box, with: □ aria-owns set to the list attribute's value

Element	Implied WAI-ARIA Role or State
	▫ with aria-readonly set to "true" if the element is readonly
input – "time" type	none, with aria-readonly set to "true" if the element is readonly
input – "URL" type	textbox, with aria-readonly set to "true" if the element is readonly
input – "week" type	none, with aria-readonly set to "true" if the element is readonly
link	link
menu – "list" type	menu
menu – "toolbar" type	toolbar
nav	navigation
option	option
progress	progressbar
select - with "multiple" attribute	listbox, with the aria-multiselectable property set to "true"
select - without "multiple" attribute	listbox, with the aria-multiselectable property set to "false"
td	gridcell
textarea	textbox
th – not a column or row header	gridcell, with the aria-labeled by property set to the value of the headers attribute, if any
th – column header	columnheader, with the aria-labelled-by property et to the value of the headers attribute, if any
th – row header	rowheader, with the aria-labelled-by property set to the value of the headers attribute, if any
tr	row

The following HTML5 elements have implied WAI-ARIA roles, but other roles may be more accurate in certain cases.

Element	Implied WAI-ARIA role	Other role option(s)
address	none	contentinfo*
article	article	article document, application, or main*
aside	note	note, complimentary, or search
body	document	document or application
footer	none	contentinfo*
header	note	banner*
li	listitem	listitem or treeitem
ol	list	list, tree, or directory
output	status	any
section	region	region, document, application, contentinfo*, main*, search, alert, dialog, alertdialog, status, log
table	grid	grid or treegrid
ul	list	list, tree, or directory

WAI-ARIA allows this role to be used only once per page.

Example

<a href="" title="Yes" role="button"><img src="yes.gif" alt="Yes"></a>

Editing and Saving Content

How do I allow users to edit content?

You can use the contenteditable attribute to allow users to edit an element's content. You can then use JavaScript or the WebStorage API to save the user's changes.

TIP *You can write the contenteditable attribute as contenteditable="true" or simply as contenteditable.*

Example

<p contenteditable="true">Beckenbauer is the best soccer player of all time.</p>

How do I save content?

You can use the WebStorage API to save content. The data is stored locally like a cookie, but you can store much more data than you can with a cookie, typically 5MB versus 2K.

The WebStorage API provides two types of storage: sessionStorage and localStorage. Data stored with sessionStorage is only available within the current window. Data stored with localStorage can be accessed if you open another window to the same domain or if you close the browser and revisit the domain.

The WebStorage API provides the following methods:

Method	Definition
clear()	Clears the entire storage object.
getItem(key)	Gets the specified key-value pair from the storage object.

Method	Definition
removeItem(key)	Removes the specified key-value pair from the storage object.
setItem(key,value)	Add the key-value pair to the storage object.

Example

The following example will save a player's first and last name.

```
<form name=myForm>
  <p><label>First Name: <input name=fName></label></p>
  <p><label>Last Name: <input name=lName></label></p>
  <input type=button value="Add Player" onclick="addPlayer()">
  <input type=button value="Get Player" onclick="getPlayer()">
  <input type=button value="Remove Player" onclick="removePlayer()">
  <table id=team></table>
  <p><label><input type=button value="Clear Team" onclick="clearAll()"></label></p>
</form>
<script>
function addPlayer() {
  var fName = document.forms.myForm.fName.value;
  var lName = document.forms.myForm.lName.value;
  localStorage.setItem(fName,lName);
  showAll();
}
function getPlayer() {
  var fName = document.forms.myForm.fName.value;
  var lName = document.forms.myForm.lName.value;
  localStorage.getItem(fName,lName);
  document.forms.myForm.fName.value = fName;
  document.forms.myForm.lName.value = lName;
  showAll();
}
function removePlayer() {
  var fName = document.forms.myForm.fName.value;
  localStorage.removeItem(fName);
  showAll();
  document.forms.myForm.fName.value = "";
  document.forms.myForm.lName.value = "";
}
function clearAll() {
  localStorage.clear();
  showAll();
}
function showAll() {
  var key = "";
```

```
var players = "<tr><th>First</th><th>Last</th></tr>\n";
var i=0;
for (i=0; i<=localStorage.length-1; i++) {
  key = localStorage.key(i);
  players += "<tr><td>"+key+"</td>\n<td>"+localStorage.getItem(key)+"</td></tr>\n";
}
if (players == "<tr><th>First</th><th>Last</th></tr>\n") {
  players += "<tr><td>empty</td>\n<td>empty</td></tr>\n";
}
document.getElementById('team').innerHTML = players;
} </script>
```

How do I view the data that has been stored using WebStorage?

You can use the following applications to view the data that has been stored on your PC/device using WebStorage:

Browser	Tool	How to Access It
Chrome	Developer Tools console	1. Click the **Page Controls** button. 2. Select **Developer** > **Developer Tools**. 3. Select **Storage**.
Firefox	Firefly plugin	firefly.mozdev.org/index.php
Internet Explorer	IE Customizer extension	iecustomizer.com/IEMenus/?txtProvider=67
Opera	Dragonfly	www.opera.com/dragonfly
Safari	Develop menu	1. Select **Edit** > **Preferences** > **Advanced** > **Show Develop menu in menu bar**. 2. Select **Develop** > **Show Web Inspector**.

Geolocation and Drag and Drop

How do I find the user's location?

You can use the Geolocation API to find the users location. You can use the getCurrentPosition() method to request permission to location the user. If the user grants permission, you can use the coords object to access the following information:

Property	Description
accuracy	The latitude and longitude measurement's accuracy in meters.
altitude	Meters above Earth.
altitudeAccuracy	The altitude's accuracy in meters.
heading	Movement from previous location in degrees clockwise from true north.
latitude	Latitude in decimal degrees.
longitude	Longitude in decimal degrees.
speed	Movement from previous location in meters/second.

The latitude, longitude, and accuracy properties should always be available. The availability of the other property values depends on the positioning server.

Example

```
<script>
function reqLoc() { navigator.geolocation.getCurrentPosition(findMe); }
function findMe(pos) {
var lat = pos.coords.latitude;
var long = pos.coords.longitude;
var acc = pos.coords.accuracy;
```

```
alert("Your latitude is: " + lat + " and your longitude is: " + long + " within " + acc + "
meters.");
}
</script>
...
<a href="javascript:void()" onClick="reqLoc()">Where am I?</a>
```

How do I use drag and drop?

You can use the draggable attribute to make an element draggable, and you can use the numerous dragging events to specify what happens when the user drags an element.

TIP *You can write the draggable attribute as draggable="true" or simply as draggable.*

Event	When It Runs
ondrag	When an element is dragged.
ondragend	At the end of a drag action.
ondragenter	When an element is dragged to a valid drop target.
ondragleave	When an element is dragged out of a valid drop target.
ondragover	When an element is dragged over a valid drop target.
ondragstart	At the start of a drag action.
ondrop	When the element is dropped.

Example

In this example, you can drag "player 1" and "player 2" into the "field" div.

```
<script>
function dragItem(target,el) { el.dataTransfer.setData('player',target.id); }
function dropItem(target,el) {
  var id = el.dataTransfer.getData('player');
  target.appendChild(document.getElementById(id));
  el.preventDefault();
}
</script>
<p draggable="true" id="p1" ondragstart="dragItem(this, event)">player 1</p>
```

```
<p draggable="true" id="p2" ondragstart="dragItem(this, event)">player 2</p>
<div id="field" style="width:500px; height:500px; background:#00c000"
ondrop="dropItem(this, event)" ondragenter="return false" ondragover="return false">
</div>
```

How do I change the cursor icon when dragging?

You can use the ondragStart event's setDragImage() method to add an icon to the cursor icon when you drag an element. It won't replace the cursor, but you can add an image like a plus sign and offset it from the cursor to visually indicate that the element is being dragged.

Example

```
var dragIcon = document.createElement('img');
dragIcon.src = "plussign.gif";
function dragItem(target,el) {
  el.dataTransfer.setData('player',target.id);
  el.dataTransfer.setDragImage(dragIcon, -10, -10);
}
```

Resources

Which software applications can I use to create HTML5 documents?

The following applications support HTML5:

- Adobe Dreamweaver CS5
- CoffeeCup's The HTML Editor 2010
- TopStyle 4

Are there any free tools I can use to create HTML5 documents?

Yes.

Mozilla Labs has created a free online HTML5 editor named Bespin. For more information, see bespin.mozilla.com/index.html. Gentics Software also has a free online HTMl5 named Aloha Editor. You can download it at www.aloha-editor.com/index.html.

How do I validate my HTML5 code?

You can use the Web Hypertext Application Technology Working Group's (WHATWG) HTML5 validator at validator.whatwg.org.

Where can I view the HTML5 recommendation?

You can view the recommendations for HTML5 and other technologies at the following sites:

Recommendation	URL
HTML5 – W3C	www.w3.org/TR/html5
HTML5 – WHATWG	www.whatwg.org/html5
Geolocation	www.w3.org/TR/geolocation-API
SVG	www.w3.org/graphics/SVG
Web Storage	www.w3.org/TR/webstorage

How can I check browser support for HMTL5?

Browser support for HMTL5 is constantly improving. You can use the following sites to check support for HMTL5's new features:

- www.caniuse.com
- www.html5test.com

How can I keep up with HTML5 changes?

You can also use the HTML5 revision tracker at www.html5.org/tools/web-apps-tracke

Can I follow HTML5 news on Twitter?

Yes. See www.twitter.com/html5.

Are there any cool HTML5 example sites on the Web?

The following websites highlight cool HTML5 examples on the Web:

- www.html5demos.com

- seogadget.co.uk/html5-examples-in-the-wild

Which HTML5 websites do you recommend?

The following websites provide excellent details about HTML5:

- www.html5doctor.com

- www.diveintohtml5.org

- www.html5gallery.com

- www.w3schools.com/html5/html5_reference.asp

HTML5 Quick Reference

The following table includes all of the supported elements in HTML5:

Element	Description	
a	A hyperlink An a element without an href attribute now represents a "placeholder link."	
abbr	Abbreviation	
address	Contact information for an article, section, or entire document.	
area	Image map region	
article	A self-contained block of content	NEW
aside	Content that is either related to the content surrounding it or the site as a whole.	NEW
audio	Inserts an audio file.	NEW
b	Text that should be "stylistically offset" but without any extra importance, such as keywords or product names.	
base	Base URL for relative links in a page	
bdo	Bi-directional text override	
blockquote	Long quotation	
body	Main content	
br	Line break	
button	Button	
canvas	An area that can contain images and shapes	NEW

Element	Description	
caption	Table caption	
cite	The title of a work *The cite element should not be used for an author or individual's name.*	
code	Code fragment	
col	Table column	
colgroup	Table column group	
command	Defines a command that can be reused	NEW
datagrid	Displays information as a tree, list, or table *The datagrid element may be removed from HTML5.*	NEW
datalist	Autocomplete options for a textbox	NEW
dd	Description of an item in a definition list (dl)	
del	Deletion	
details	Shows and hides content	NEW
dfn	Definition of a term	
dialog	A quoted conversation *The dialog element may be removed from HTML5.*	NEW
div	Generic division	
dl	Definition list	
dt	Definition term	
em	Emphasis	

Element	Description	
embed	An application or other interactive content	NEW
eventsource	Specifies an external source for a script or a web-based application	NEW
fieldset	Form control	NEW
figcaption	A caption for a figure	NEW
figure	Content that is referenced from the main content but could be moved to the side of the page	
footer	An author's name, links to related documents, or a copyright statement	NEW
form	Form for user input	
h1-h6	Heading level 1-6	
head	Document head	
header	A document or section heading, a section's table of contents, a search form, or a logo	NEW
hgroup	A section's heading	NEW
hr	Horizontal rule (i.e., a line) or a paragraph-level thematic break	
html	Document root	
i	Text in an alternate voice or mood, or otherwise "stylistically offset," such as a technical term.	
iframe	Inline frame	
img	Image	
input	Form control	
ins	Inserted text	
kbd	Text to be typed by the user ('keyboard')	

Element	Description	
keygen	Generates a public-private key pair	NEW
label	Input element label	
legend	Fieldset caption	
li	List item	
link	Link to a resource such as a stylesheet	
map	Client-side image map	
mark	Emphasized content in a quote that was not emphasized by the original author, or emphasized content that is most likely relevant to the user	NEW
menu	A toolbar, context menu, or list of commands	NEW
meta	Information about the document ('metadata')	
meter	Allows a user to select an amount within a set range	NEW
nav	A document's primary navigation links	NEW
noscript	Alternative content for no script support	
object	Generic embedded resource	
ol	Ordered list	
optgroup	Groups items in a drop-down listbox	NEW
optgroup	Option group in a select list	
option	An option in a select list	
output	Displays the results of a calculation	NEW
p	Paragraph	
param	Parameters for an object or applet	

Element	Description	
pre	Preformatted text	
progress	Indicates when an event will be completed.	NEW
q	Inline quotation	
ruby rt rp	Provide a pronunciation guide or translation	NEW
samp	Sample code output	
script	Linked or embedded script	
section	Self-contained block of content	NEW
select	Selection (i.e., drop-down) list	
small	Small print for side comments and legal text	
source	Alternate audio or video file	NEW
span	Generic inline container	
strong	Strong importance ◇ *This element no longer represents strong emphasis or boldfacing.*	
style	Embedded styles declaration block	
sub	Subscript	
summary	The legend (i.e., title) of a details element	NEW
sup	Superscript	
table	Table	
tbody	Table body	
td	Table data cell	

Element	Description	
textarea	Multi-line text box	
tfoot	Table footer	
th	Table header cell	
thead	Table head	
time	A date and time	NEW
title	Document title	
tr	Table row	
ul	Unordered (i.e., bulleted) list	
var	Variable	
video	Inserts a video file.	NEW
wbr	A line break "opportunity"	NEW

Index

Training

ClickStart offers training and consulting for MadCap Flare, Adobe Captivate, CSS, and HTML. You can also sign-up for our email newsletter. For more information, visit our website at **www.clickstart.net**.